Having Fun
PRINTING

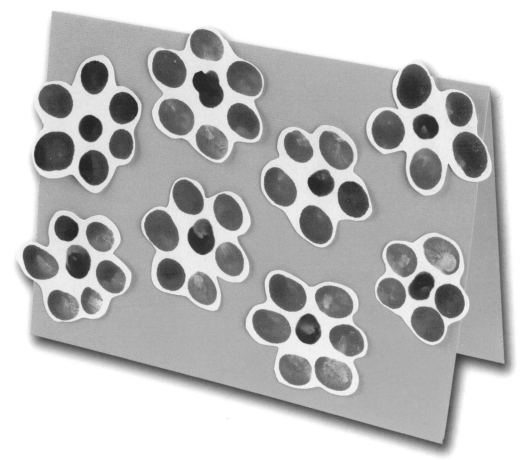

Sarah Medina

WAYLAND

First published in 2007 by Wayland
This paperback edition published in 2011 by Wayland

Wayland
338 Euston Road
London NW1 3BH

Wayland
Level 17/207 Kent Street
Sydney, NSW 2000

Medina, Sarah
  Having fun with printing. – (Let's do art)
  1. Printing – Technique – Juvenile literature
  I. Title
  760.2'8

Written by Sarah Medina
Produced by Calcium
Design and model making by Emma DeBanks
Photography by Tudor Photography
Consultancy and concepts by Lisa Regan

ISBN 978-0-7502-6524-9

Printed in China

Wayland is a division of Hachette Children's Books,
an Hachette UK Company
www.hachette.co.uk

Contents

Printing Fun!   4

Poppy Field   6

Street Scene   8

Money Tube   10

People Print   12

On the Moon   14

Come to My Party!   16

Noughts and Crosses   18

Happy-Sad Clown   20

Further Ideas   23
Further Information   24
Glossary   24
Index   24

Printing Fun!

Printing uses different objects, such as vegetables and household items, to make a picture. These are the kinds of materials you will need:

- Cling film
- Foil paper
- Empty crisp or biscuit tube with a lid
- Household items (drinking straws, corks, plastic cups, knife and spoon)
- Metallic paints
- Paintbrush
- Paper
- Plastic bottle

- Poster paints
- String
- Vegetables (potatoes, courgettes and carrots)
- Wax crayons
- White and coloured card and cardboard

Note for adults
Children may need adult assistance with some of the project steps. Turn to page 23 for Further Ideas.

Read the 'You will need' boxes carefully for a full list of what you need to make each project.

Before you start, ask an adult to:

- find a surface where you can make the projects.

- find an apron to cover your clothes, or some old clothes that can get messy.

- do things, such as cutting with scissors, that are a little tricky to do on your own.

Poppy Field

Use a bottle and string to create a fabulous nature print.

You will need

- 1 plastic bottle
- 1 long piece of string
- Cling film
- 1 sheet of paper
- Paintbrushes
- Poster paints – including green and red
- PVA glue

1 Using the paintbrush, brush thin lines of glue in circles all around the bottle.

2 Wrap string around the bottle where you have brushed on the glue. Leave to dry.

3 Brush green paint onto a large piece of cling film.

4 Roll the bottle lightly over the paint and then roll it over the paper. Repeat until you have created plenty of grass on the field!

5 When the green paint is dry, paint red poppies onto your print.

Street Scene

Design a building and use it to make a street scene!

1 Draw a roof shape, and squares and rectangles of different sizes on sheets of card. Cut them out.

2 Glue the shapes onto cardboard, with some of them on top of others, to make a building with doors and windows. Leave to dry.

3 Place a sheet of paper over the building.

4 Starting at the left side of the paper, rub a wax crayon over the building.

5 Move the paper across and rub wax crayon over the building again. Repeat to print lots of buildings!

 Ask an adult for help with cutting card!

9

Money Tube

Save your spare coins in
a printed money tube!

You will need

- An empty crisp or biscuit tube, with a lid
- Cork
- Metallic paints
- I sheet of coloured paper
- Paintbrush
- PVA glue
- Scissors

1 Cut the paper so
that it fits around
the tube and then
lay the paper flat.

 Ask an adult
for help with
cutting paper!

10

2 Dip one end of the cork into metallic paint and press it onto the paper to print a coin.

3 Print more coins in this colour onto the paper.

4 Repeat steps 2 and 3 using different paint colours, and leave to dry.

5 Brush glue all over the tube and glue the paper onto it. Put the lid on.

People Print

Create a picture of a person using items from the kitchen!

1 Pour different coloured paints into foil trays.

2 Dip the edge of the cup into paint and press onto the paper to print a face.

12

3 Dip the plastic knife into paint and print hair around the face.

4 Dip the end of the straw into paint and print eyes and a nose on the face.

5 Dip the long edge of the end of a spoon into paint and print a smiling mouth on the face.

On the Moon

Fly to the moon with this space-age project!

You will need

- Card
- 1 large sheet of black paper
- Foil paper
- Black felt-tip pen
- Poster paints – light brown, orange and yellow
- PVA glue
- Scissors

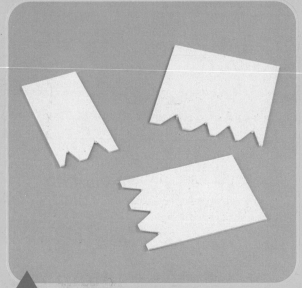

1 Cut three rectangles of card in different sizes and cut small triangles into one edge of each of the cards.

 Ask an adult for help with cutting card!

4 Draw craters and mountains onto the moon.

2 Dip the cut edge of the largest rectangle into light brown paint and drag it across the paper. Allow to dry.

3 Using the other two rectangles, repeat step 2 using orange paint and then yellow paint.

5 Cut a spaceship and some stars from foil paper, and glue them onto the picture.

Come to My Party!

Use your unique fingerprints to make flowery party invitations!

1 Dip your finger into paint and press down on the paper to make the centres of the flowers. Print lots of flower petals in another colour around them.

2 Cut out the flowers.

3 Fold sheets of coloured card in half for your invitations.

4 Arrange the flowers all over the card and glue into place.

5 Now write your party invitations!

 Ask an adult for help with cutting paper!

Noughts and Crosses

Make a fun game to play with a friend!

1 Dip the straw into black paint and press it onto the card to make lines for the board.

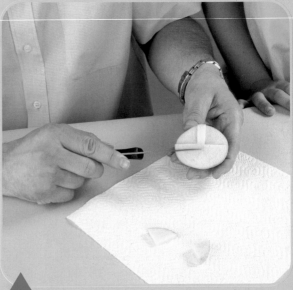

2 Draw a cross on a potato half and ask an adult to cut the potato so the cross stands out.

3 Draw a circle on a potato half and ask an adult to cut the potato so the circle stands out.

4 Dip the potato cross into paint, press it onto paper five times and cut the crosses out.

5 Dip the potato circle into paint, press it onto paper five times and cut the circles out.

 Ask an adult for help with cutting!

Happy-Sad Clown

Have fun making this happy-sad clown's face!

You will need

- 1 half of a courgette (cut lengthways)
- 2 halves of a carrot
- 2 halves of a potato
- 1 sheet of card
- 1 large sheet of paper
- 1 paper fastener
- Black felt-tip pen
- Foil tray
- Knife
- Poster paints
- Scissors

1 Draw a circle on a large sheet of paper to make the clown's face.

2 Ask an adult to cut a carrot in half. Dip one end into paint and print hair around the face.

4 Dip the other potato half into paint and print a nose on the face.

5 Cut a courgette in half lengthways and dip it into paint. Print a mouth onto card and leave to dry.

3 Draw a cross on a potato half and ask an adult to cut the potato so the cross stands out. Dip the cross into paint and print two eyes on the face.

 Ask an adult for help with cutting!

6 Cut the mouth from the card. Using a paper fastener, attach the mouth to the clown's face. Turn the mouth up to make a happy clown or turn it down to make a sad clown.

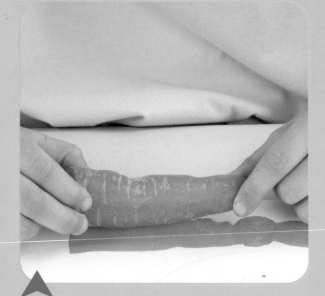

7 Ask an adult to cut a carrot in half lengthways. Dip the potato half and the long edge of the carrot half into paint, and print a bow tie under the clown's face.

Further Ideas

Once a child has finished the projects in *Having Fun with Printing*, they can add some other exciting finishing touches to them.

Poppy Field
Cut out pictures of bees and other insects from magazines, and glue them onto the picture.

Street Scene
Use a black felt-tip pen to draw small people and cars onto the street in your scene.

Money Tube
Ask an adult to cut a slot in the lid for money to go in.

People Print
Make a hat using felt and sequins, and glue it onto the portrait.

On the Moon
Cut out a picture of an astronaut from a magazine, or print one from the Internet, and add it to the moonscape.

Come to my Party!
Glue sequins onto the flower petals to make them sparkle!

Noughts and Crosses
Use the potato circles and crosses to print a border around the board.

Happy-Sad Clown
Cut a flower shape out of half a potato, dip it into paint and print a flower onto the clown's head.

Further Information

With access to the Internet, you can check out several helpful websites for further arts and crafts ideas for young children.

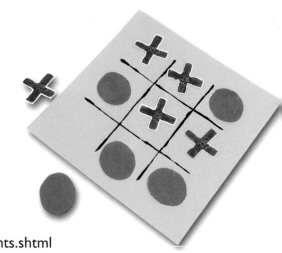

www.kidsart.com/q_snowman.html
www.theideabox.com/Autumn_Tree.html
www.brightring.com/blottos.html
www.dltk-kids.com/animals/handprint.htm
www.amazingmoms.com/htm/artpainting.htm#marble_paint
www.bbc.co.uk/cbeebies/artbox/artisttips/feature/monster_prints.shtml

Glossary

border a decoration all around the edge of a piece of work

metallic shiny and sparkly, like silver or gold

poster paint paint made with a kind of glue, which dries quickly and gives bright colours

print to transfer colour on to paper or card using an object such as a potato, a straw or a cork

scenes places that you can recognize

Index

adult help 3, 23
clown 20–22
finger printing 16
flowers 6–7, 16
money tube 10–11
moonscape 14–15
noughts and crosses 18–19
party invitation 16–17
portrait 12–13
potato printing 18–19, 20–22
street scene 8–9
vegetable printing 20–22